Restructuring Schools

The Practicing Administrator's Leadership Series
Jerry J. Herman and Janice L. Herman, Editors

ROADMAPS TO SUCCESS

Other Titles in This Series Include:

The Path to School Leadership
A Portable Mentor
Lee G. Bolman and Terrence E. Deal

Holistic Quality
Managing, Restructuring, and Empowering Schools
Jerry J. Herman

Selecting, Managing, and Marketing Technologies
Jamieson A. McKenzie

Individuals With Disabilities
Implementing the Newest Laws
Patricia F. First and Joan L. Curcio

Violence in the Schools
How to Proactively Prevent and Defuse It
Joan L. Curcio and Patricia F. First

Women in Administration
Facilitators for Change
L. Nan Restine

Power Learning in the Classroom
Jamieson A. McKenzie

Conflict Resolution
Building Bridges
Neil Katz

Computers: Literacy and Learning
A Primer for Administrators
George E. Marsh II

Dealing With Gangs
A Handbook for Administrators
Shirley R. Lal, Dhyan Lal, and Charles M. Achilles

Restructuring Schools

Doing It Right

Mike M. Milstein

CORWIN PRESS, INC.
A Sage Publications Company
Newbury Park, California

For information address:

Corwin Press, Inc.
A Sage Publications Company
2455 Teller Road
Newbury Park, California 91320

SAGE Publications Ltd.
6 Bonhill Street
London EC2A 4PU
United Kingdom

SAGE Publications India Pvt. Ltd.
M-32 Market
Greater Kailash I
New Delhi 110 048 India

Printed in the United States of America

Library of Congress Cataloging-in-Publication Data

Milstein, Mike M.
    Restructuring schools: doing it right / by Mike M. Milstein.
        p.   cm.—(Roadmaps to success)
    Includes bibliographical references (p.   ).
    ISBN 0-8039-6072-7
    1. School improvement programs—United States.   2. School
management and organization—United States.   I. Title.   II. Series.
LB2822.82.M55   1993
371.2'00973—dc20   93-17872

93 94 95 96 10 9 8 7 6 5 4 3 2 1

Corwin Press Production Editor: Marie Louise Penchoen

Contents

Foreword

In *Restructuring Schools: Doing It Right*, Mike Milstein addresses the origins, purposes, and methods of restructuring schools—and clarifies what is meant by *restructuring*. In addition, he calls for a necessary overall change in thinking about our approach to education.

Milstein outlines activities that promote restructuring, presents information on the means of developing structures and roles to accomplish restructuring, and explores reasons why creating change in schools is a very difficult task. Finally, he offers methods to assess the effectiveness of restructuring efforts.

One of the outstanding features of this book is a graphic model that also forms the structure of the text. All of the elements in the model are interrelated and when properly combined lead to excellence, equity, and effectiveness in education. An annotated bibliography and listing of significant references complete this practical and timely book.

JERRY J. HERMAN
JANICE L. HERMAN
Series Co-Editors

About the Author

Mike Milstein has been actively engaged in school restructuring. He has facilitated an urban school district's restructuring team, provided guidance for a rural school district's administrative team, and helped many schools develop structures, modify roles, and learn necessary skills in the pursuit of restructuring.

Milstein is Professor of Educational Administration, Division of Innovative Programs, at the University of New Mexico. Prior to this position, he was a professor of educational administration at SUNY/Buffalo. His teaching, research, and writing interests are in the area of organization development. Most recently, he has focused his energies on educator plateauing and resilience.

Restructuring: What Is It?

School districts are being encouraged to *restructure*, but as with most buzz words, restructuring is coming to have different meaning for different people. This can cause all sorts of difficulties when school districts contemplate undertaking restructuring initiatives. The purpose of this chapter is to help you develop a clearer understanding of what restructuring is so you can decide whether you are ready and willing to begin such efforts. I present here a working definition of restructuring and framework which divides restructuring activities into four elements and organizes the structure of this book.

Why Restructure?

The rush toward educational restructuring has its genesis in earlier efforts to improve the performance of the country's economy by changing the way our commercial and industrial organizations operate. Capturing the tone of that effort, the authors of the path-finding book *In Search of Excellence* note:

At a gut level all of us know that much more goes into the process of keeping a large organization vital and responsive than the policy statements, new strategies, plans, budgets, and organization charts can possibly depict. But all too often we behave as though we don't know it. If we want change, we fiddle with the strategy. Or we change the structure. Perhaps the time has come to change our ways. (Peters & Waterman, 1982, p. 3)

Both the impetus for restructuring educational systems and the reform movement of the 1980s occurred against this societal backdrop. During the first half of the decade, various public and private reports (see, for example, National Commission on Excellence in Education, 1983; Carnegie Forum, 1986) drew a stark picture of our public schools' performance in educating the nation's youth. By the end of the decade, the image being portrayed was one of a failing educational system:

The rapidly changing global society and economy require a very different worker and citizen than the schools are now graduating. Indeed, the existing system is unable to prepare the graduates our country needs. The high percentage of dropouts, the large number of failing students hidden behind the mean scores on standardized tests, and the graduates who are not ready for work or additional learning constitute an embarrassing testimony. Many students leave school without even minimal skills. (*National LEADership Network*, 1991, p. 7)

Broad scale public debate led to many state-level policy initiatives aimed at reforming school districts. "By the mid-1980s, over 200 state-level task forces, blue ribbon commissions, and study groups, were at work around the country. . . . The large scale reforms enacted in 15 to 20 states in the first years of the reform movement transformed education—not just in those states, but in all states" (Pipho, 1992, pp. 278-279).

These "top-down" mandates covered a wide spectrum of reforms: for example, the length of the school day, the minimum time to be devoted to specific subject matter, the maximum number of students in classrooms, and changes in licensure requirements for teachers and administrators. Many of these initiatives were not funded adequately. In fact, it was not long before state-level policymakers realized that they could not raise the necessary resources and they quietly withdrew from the arena.

This left responsibility for reform in the hands of the very same school districts that were criticized as not being equal to the task. With demands to "do something" remaining high, but with little agreement about goals or provision of means to guide the effort, leaders of school districts across the country found that the ball was squarely back in their court. Efforts undertaken by school leaders to respond came to be called *restructuring,* which is "distinguished as much by its philosophical underpinnings as it is by its structural or operational components. Its most salient characteristics are influenced by a belief system and a vision that require radically different responses to the problems of education than are possible within current forms of schooling" (*National LEADership Network*, 1991, p. 8).

During the 1980s, public school reform increased dramatically. By the end of the decade, a shift had occurred from the external call for reform at the outset of the decade to efforts to restructure the system from the inside.

Restructuring Defined

I define *restructuring* here as *systemic change or transformation with the intent of improving educational effectiveness in ways that meet the changing needs of our society.* Systemic change means that restructuring is *comprehensive: All* aspects of the system, including mission, goals, structures, policies, roles, participation, and relationships are candidates for change because they impact *what* is taught (curricular content), *how* it is presented (instructional delivery), and *where* it occurs (the setting).

Because of the variety of situations existing in the 50 states, the more than 16,000 school districts, and the countless number of schools that constitute public education in the United States, the specific emphasis of particular restructuring efforts will vary widely. However, underlying these diverse situations lies a basic principle: *Restructuring efforts should focus on reducing the disparity between current educational outcomes and educational outcomes required to prepare today's students to meet the challenges of tomorrow's world.*

Key Restructuring Elements

What is restructuring? The U.S. Department of Education (*National LEADership Network*, 1991) views programs and services for students, roles and relationships, rules and regularities, and accountability as the key elements. Murphy (1991) suggests three categories—work roles, governance structures, and the core technology. Lieberman and Miller (1990) see restructuring as including rethinking curriculum, instructional efforts and structures, focus on rich learning environments for students and adults, recognition of the need to build partnerships and networks, and recognition of increased and changing participation of parents and community. Bailey's review (1992) of 16 restructuring authors identifies many elements—the most frequently mentioned being decentralization (12), professionalism (10), empowerment (9), student learning (7), accountability (5), and uses of time (5). Although specific restructuring elements differ across these authors, all are similar in that they emphasize *improved educational outcomes* and suggest that purposes, processes, structures, and roles *must all be rethought* for this to happen.

The key restructuring elements most frequently noted in the literature are shown in Figure 1.1. *Effective Education* characterized by *Excellence and Equity* is at the center of this figure. This is what restructuring is all about—assuring *that all students, minorities and the disabled as well as the average and gifted, have equal access to a good education and that the content and its delivery are well conceived and presented.* Everything done in the name of restructuring should be measured against this template: Will it have a positive impact on the education students receive?

In pursuit of these outcomes, I have distinguished four major elements (each of these is represented as one of the quadrants in Figure 1.1):

Figure 1.1. The key elements of restructuring.

1. *Purposes* must be examined, modified, and clarified:
   a. The *mission* of the school district and the schools within it need to be examined and, as necessary, altered to reflect the changing realities of our shrinking world.
   b. Clearly-stated and agreed-on *goals* that support the mission and provide clarity and direction for restructuring efforts must be developed.
   c. *Long-term perspectives* of 5 to 10 years and the patience to stay the course through the inevitable lean times are required to increase the potential of institutionalizing restructuring efforts.
   d. *Assessment and accountability* systems must be created and implemented to provide evidence of movement

toward goal achievement and to remind those who participate about their responsibilities to monitor outcomes.

2. *Structures and Roles* must be altered in ways that promote the achievement of the purposes:

   a. *Decentralization*—a significant reduction of state-level oversight of school district activities as well as school district oversight of school-level activities has to be implemented. The intent is to remove bureaucratic restrictions and hierarchical controls, both of which tend to inhibit motivation, ownership, and creativity at the school-site level.

   b. *Site-based management* must be pursued so participants will have opportunities to come together to sort through the school's needs and develop creative responses to them.

   c. *Widespread involvement* opens the way for meaningful contributions by key groups, including teachers and other school-site personnel, parents and other community members, business leaders, and students.

   d. *Participative decision making*, combined with the other structural changes, can lead to a sense of empowerment.

3. Specific *Beliefs and Behaviors* must be promoted to help everyone involved clarify and modify expectations and become more skilled and effective in achieving missions and goals:

   a. *Skill development* has to be promoted to enhance the potential of effective interactions. These skills relate to *governance* (for example, goal setting, problem solving, meeting management, and conflict management) and to *effective education* (for example, curriculum development; classroom management; and instructional delivery that supports concepts such as the teacher as coach and the student as worker, higher order thinking skills, and cooperative approaches to learning).

   b. *Teamwork and cooperation* must be promoted because creative approaches to effective education are more likely to be forthcoming through cooperation than through competition.

   c. *Trust and risk taking* need to be promoted as empowerment is pursued through participation and cooperation.

   d. *Ownership* must be promoted so that all partners see the process as a win-win situation and restructuring efforts can take hold.

4. *Resources* must be identified and allocated to provide necessary support for the effort:

   a. *Money* is needed for a variety of activities, including skill development, curriculum development, alternative instructional delivery systems, and participative management arrangements.

   b. Because *people* ultimately make restructuring work, staff, students, parents, and other community members have to be motivated to participate in the effort as cooperative partners.

   c. *Space* may need to be added, or at least modified, to promote changes in governance structures and instructional delivery systems.

   d. *Time* is needed for participants to meet to agree on purposes, establish plans, put them into operation, and monitor outcomes.

Earlier in the chapter restructuring was described as "systemic" and "comprehensive." Given the mission of restructuring—namely, "improving educational effectiveness in ways that meet the changing needs of our society"—we need to do better. However, recent studies indicate that "even where restructuring is taking hold, for the most part it is doing so in a piecemeal way. It is difficult to find schools in the nation that have comprehensively restructured education" (Center on Organization and Restructuring of Schools, 1992).

The Potential Payoff

We are in uncharted waters. Restructuring is a systemic approach to change, an approach that is much more complex than anything done before. Why should you consider pursuing such a complex and pervasive effort as restructuring? The most important reason is that *restructuring has the potential of improving the education of students in ways that enable them to cope more successfully in a rapidly changing world. It also has the potential of increasing educators' sense of job satisfaction and feeling of professionalism and of enhancing the likelihood of positive partnerships between schools, parents, and the general community.* However, to realize potentials, restructuring must be effective. This requires that all of the systemic aspects of restructuring as represented in Figure 1.1 must be well managed.

In Closing

The purposes of this book are 1) to help you diagnose whether your systems have the potential of successfully initiating restructuring efforts and 2) to present strategies for introducing and institutionalizing restructuring purposes successfully if the effort is made. The book divides roughly into two parts: The first part defines restructuring (Chapter 1) and then with a chapter for each describes in some detail the four quadrants of Figure 1.1—purposes (Chapter 2), structures and roles (Chapter 3), beliefs and behaviors (Chapter 4), and resources (Chapter 5). The second part explores the processes of change involved in restructuring (Chapter 6), examining the process of assessing the effort (Chapter 7), and presenting activities to help facilitate the restructuring process (Chapter 8).

Clarifying Purposes

If the school organization is not to continue doing what it has always done—and continue getting the same results it always has—then you must clarify the purposes of restructuring. Meaningful plans for change and improvement require serious thought about where you want to go. Therefore, initial restructuring activities must focus on developing a clear set of directions that can provide a driving force for partnership building and programs that implement what you believe students need to know and be able to do. This chapter examines the Purposes section of Figure 1.1—mission, goals, long-term perspectives, and accountability. These areas are defined and explored from two perspectives, the overall school district and the individual school.

Mission

The mission of an organization is its overall charge or calling. Unfortunately, many organizations do not clarify their missions. Others develop bland or pious mission statements that do not provide a sense of purpose or stimulate participants to contribute to the effort. Clarity and agreement about a mission statement can help an organization establish what is required to move beyond survival and toward excellence. The *re* in restructuring implies that school districts must examine and state their missions anew in the light of changing societal conditions in order to be perceived as relevant and effective.

Here are some important activities that need to be conducted in developing a mission.

Environmental Scanning. Gathering information and mobilizing all partners to cooperate in the process is a necessary beginning. You need to gather information that helps you understand trends and probable futures—national, state, and local demographic information such as socioeconomic, racial, and ethnic migration trends; likely shifts in the global, national, state, and local economy; likely changes in the dynamics of the home, church, and other relevant agencies; and societal shifts in values and beliefs.

Deriving Meaning and Establishing Priorities. Processing the results of the environmental scan is as important for the process as it is for the results. The partners (school board members, administrators, teachers, and other members of the system, along with students, parents, and other community members) should participate in the analysis and agree on the meaning for education. If this happens, the process is likely to lead to meaningful mission statements as well as broad understanding, commitment, and support from all sides for restructuring efforts that flow from these statements.

Creating a Mission Statement. A mission statement should be focused and behaviorally anchored. Care must be taken to craft statements that have the potential to guide decision making and set priorities for resource allocation. Mission statements that are platitudes—such as, "All students will become all that they can become"—do not provide the guidelines for actions that focused mission statements—such as, "Offer all students opportunities to excel in their education"—do.

At the District Level

Pursuit of a mission statement requires that the school board become actively involved. Board members are the community's representatives, so their understanding and support of the mission is important. This is more likely to be achieved if they participate in the development of the mission statement, which may require that the board "retreat" for a block of time, perhaps several days, to explore results of the environmental scan and develop a consensus about the mission statement.

The central office administrative team also must be part of the process. You need the solid support and backing of this group of leaders because they are the messengers who will send positive or negative signals about the district's mission to those at the school-site level. Efforts need to be made to develop a highly skilled central office team that can play a key leadership role in motivating others to conduct activities in pursuit of the mission statement.

At the School-Site Level

School-site leaders must participate in establishing the district mission statement. You have important inputs to offer and your understanding and support of the mission is critical if positive follow-through activities are to occur. You also must be charged with the responsibility to work with your own professional staff and lay community to specify missions for school sites that are supportive of the district mission. Time has to be reserved to stimulate a dialog among staff members from the school site, along with students, parents, and other community members, with the intent of creating a site-specific mission that will guide goal-setting and restructuring activities.

Goals

Goals are ideals—or statements of where organizations want to be. If done well, they specify ways that the organization intends to fulfill its mission and motivate the partners to devote time and energy to that mission. As such, goals should 1) be clear, so they can be understood; 2) be attractive to those who will be asked to participate; 3) be challenging yet within the organization's capacity to realize; 4) be capable of being measured, to test the extent to which they are being achieved; and 5) leave participants feeling positive about working together toward goal fulfillment.

If goals are to provide motivation for growth and change they must include statements that span three time periods.

Long-Term Goals. Long-term goals identify where the organization ultimately wants to be. They provide a sense of purpose, setting overarching directions to move the organization toward the fulfillment of its mission. Such goals take years of concentrated effort to achieve. For example, given the rapidly changing world in which we live, this might be a long-term goal: "Enable students to gain the ability to think critically and demonstrate that ability after they leave school and become members of the adult community."

Mid-Range Goals. These goals are marking posts supportive of long-term goals. They provide a motivational base for participants because they can be recognized when they are attained. For example, in pursuit of critical thinking, it is important to set midterm goals such as, "By the end of their 7th-grade year, students in American History will be able to develop alternative theories of the evolution of democracy in the United States."

Short-Range Goals. These are akin to stepping stones. They are time framed tightly, usually within a few weeks or a few months, and they are easily identifiable. Following the example above, this might be a short-term goal: "Students will be able to synthesize the main lessons that the colonists learned about representative governance as they confronted the British in the 1770s." Accomplishment of short-term goals gives participants a sense of movement. They also allow organizations to measure with specificity the extent to which mid-range and long-range goals are being supported. Care needs to be taken that short-term goals do not become so narrow and bounded that they lead to measuring triviality.

Those involved in the goal-setting process must be sure to 1) connect goals to the mission statement; 2) state goals behaviorally so they can be measured; 3) limit their numbers so follow-up efforts are focused and relevant rather than dissipated and superficial; and, given the rapidly changing environment we live in, 4) review and update them regularly.

At the District Level

Once a mission statement is developed, the board, administrative leadership, and involved community members would benefit by engaging in goal-setting exercises that identify districtwide priorities over the next 5 to 10 years. If done effectively, this process can lend specificity to the mission, establish understandings and agreements, create a basis for decision making about scarce resources, and provide guidance for school-site goal setting.

At the School-Site Level

Within the context of districtwide goal statements, a similar goal-setting process can clarify future actions at the school site. Again, widespread involvement will increase the likelihood of creating comprehensive goals that will be understood, agreed on, and pursued.

Long-Term Perspectives

Restructuring is not Band-Aiding! School districts are notorious for their predilection to generic and packaged "solutions" that focus on quick fixes. Inevitably this approach falls short as a response to pervasive problem situations.

It took a long time to get where we are, and it will take a long time to get where we want to go! It will also take recognition that there is no easy or short-term solution. Rather, there must be a comprehensive and systemic approach as well as the willingness to stay the course for the long haul. A conservative estimate is that you should expect to devote a minimum of 5 to 10 years to make significant changes in the purposes of public education and the processes employed to achieve these purposes (Fullan, 1991). Clarifying purposes, agreeing on processes, establishing necessary resources, involving the partners in the effort, assessing effectiveness, and creating necessary modifications are all time-consuming activities—which are likely to be encountered more than once in the effort! Rushing the process and taking shortcuts may appear attractive and more efficient, but history has taught us that changing an organization's culture and institutionalizing innovations takes time.

Restructuring should be viewed as an ongoing process that will never be completed, at least as long as we live in a dynamically changing world. Recognizing the complexity and difficulty of institutional change, you need to develop long-term perspectives. Metaphorically speaking, changing organizations is like trying to change the course of an ocean liner: shifting the steering mechanism even 1 degree will, in due time, lead the ship to make major changes in its direction.

The notion of long-term perspectives has implications for leadership behaviors. First, as noted, you need to resist chasing after "quick fix" solutions, which are usually doomed to failure. Even worse, they leave those involved feeling guilt for the failure and less willing to participate in the next change campaign. Second, you need to help the partners develop a common vision, operationalized as a mission statement and a set of supportive goals, and then act as the spokesperson who effectively communicates the results of the effort to all participants. Communication must occur many times and through various approaches—orally, in writing, and by any other means possible. Third, you must have the courage to stay the course. As noted in Chapter 6, there will be opposition to major change efforts, and there will likely be "failures" along the way when significant changes are tried. You must set the tone and model risk taking if you expect others to do so.

At the District Level

The school board and administration need to learn about the realities of organizational change. There is a growing literature about this phenomenon, both from the private sector and from the education sector (for example, Chin & Benne, 1969; Fullan, 1991; Hall & Hord, 1987; Kanter, 1989), that should be reviewed and internalized to foster realistic perspectives about change dynamics. Further, given the widespread nature of school district restructuring, it is incumbent on you to become familiar with what is going on elsewhere, focusing particularly on extremes—that is, examples of effective and ineffective restructuring efforts. Because many school districts are involved with restructuring efforts, much of what you need to know is likely being experimented with some place. In this sense, restructuring is a search process as often as it is an invention process. Finally, past district change efforts should be reviewed to learn from them. Were they dropped or institutionalized? What happened? What mattered?

At the School-Site Level

School leaders must become familiar with the dynamics of organizational change. You must have the skill and the desire to bring other adults—both staff members and community members—together as partners who become committed to improving the education of students and who recognize that they will be involved in the effort for the long haul. District leaders can help by setting up professional development opportunities for site leaders that focus on this phenomenon. Site leaders also should be encouraged to visit other schools that are making progress on important changes. Such visits can provide ideas and the stimulus to take risks. If the schools that are visited are outside the district, it is more likely you will see the change effort there as an opportunity rather than as a threat, which might occur if you observe changes at one of your colleagues' schools in the district. Having acted as a scout, you can then return as a harbinger of new ideas.

Accountability

Establishing a culture that promotes accountability, taking responsibility and being answerable for actions, is one of the most revolutionary—and therefore most likely to be resisted—of the concepts associated with restructuring. State departments of education are relaxing regulatory activities through such actions as waivers, and district-level administrators are reducing oversight efforts, encouraging site-based budgeting and site-based management. However, as opportunities for taking initiatives move to school sites, there is also great expectation that the sites will be held accountable for results.

The need for accountability has widespread agreement, but what it means and how it should function are less clear. Further, those who are going to be held accountable are understandably concerned about taking on this obligation, partly because there is little clarity about what it means or how to do it and partly because it requires additional efforts that may lead to the judgment that outcomes are inadequate. Accountability is not really as mysterious as many believe. Simply put, it is "a process of providing information to others, enabling judgments to be made" (Caldwell & Spinks, 1992, p. 139). Evaluation approaches that can be helpful in meeting accountability demands are explored in Chapter 7.

At the District Level

You need to develop realistic expectations about accountability and help site-level personnel understand why it is necessary. You also need to set specific expectations based on the district's mission and goal statements and to provide assessment approaches as well as professional development opportunities that help site-based leaders become knowledgeable about accountability methods and how to use them. Setting expectations and providing training and support can enhance the ability of school sites to meet demands for accountability. If these activities are done in a supportive way rather than in a controlling manner, it is more likely that accountability activities will be viewed as a natural part of the process of moving toward goals.

At the School-Site Level

You need to acquaint your staff and the community with the importance of assessment information as feedback to the planning and implementation process. You also must lobby for the fiscal and human resources required to help these partners become more knowledgeable and skillful in conducting assessment-related activities. Once assessment information becomes available in an understandable manner, you can make necessary changes in your strategies to keep restructuring efforts on course.

In Closing

If significant progress can be made "up front" in the early stages of restructuring effort, the activities that need to be initiated for the other sectors of Figure 1.1 will be more manageable. With purposes established and agreed on by the partners, you will be in a much better position to make decisions regarding structures and roles, the focus of the next chapter.

Developing Structures and Roles
to Serve Purposes

Why is there so much interest in changing the ways we structure our schools and conduct activities in them? Recent research indicates that "schools attempting restructuring make changes in teaching techniques, but negligibly few schools are embarking upon changes in governance and relationships with the larger community" (Center on Organization, 1992, p. 4). This should concern us because how we organize and relate to each other can make a big difference in our ability to fulfill missions and goals. This chapter explores the need for school districts that are contemplating restructuring to implement structural and role changes, including decentralization, site-based management, widespread involvement, and participative decision making.

Structure and Role Changes: Important Considerations

First and foremost, *anything done to change the structure of the organization and the roles of the partners should be directly related to the improvement of students' education.* The idea is not to create elegant structures that capture our fancy or impress others with our creativity and risk-taking propensity. Rather, it is to facilitate the achievement of the educational mission and goals. Everything should emanate from the purpose of improving educational outcomes. This criterion should be used as the template for judging efforts to change the system.

Second, structural changes are based on the assumption that *the partners need to be empowered if they are going to create the capacity for change*. Students, teachers, administrators, parents, and other community members need access to the system if they are going to influence it. This requires that the system be reconfigured in ways that change the balance of power and provide seats at the decision-making table for partners who previously did not have one.

Third, *major changes in roles and role relationships will have to take place*. Structural changes will have little impact on educational outcomes unless major efforts are also made to legitimize the involvement of diverse groups by redefining roles and role relationships. Students have to be viewed as active partners in the system who have a voice in the creation and implementation of learning situations rather than as passive vessels to be filled; parents and other community members have to be viewed as active partners who have a unique role to play in the process; the input of teachers will have to be expanded beyond their instructional role in the classroom to include involvement in the policy-making and governance arena; and administrators will have to become facilitators who keep the partners on target rather than act as traditional leaders who rely on hierarchical authority positions for power.

Finally, because these suggestions represent radical changes in structures and roles, *expectations need to be agreed on and written in clear and operational language, and accountability for results must be established*. Experimentation with different structures and role relationships must be encouraged to deal with different situations. However, because of this reality of diversity, standards for performance and results must be set at the outset. These standards should be based on the educational mission and goals. They should also relate to agreements about decentralization, site-based management, widespread involvement, and participative decision making.

Decentralization

Centralized systems are based on the belief that a high level of control is needed to assure that minimal fulfillment of expectations will be achieved by those at the service level of the organization. On the contrary, "decentralization requires that you believe in your fellow human beings" (Brown, 1991, p. 108). In fact, the assumption behind decentralization is that, compared to those at distant administrative centers, partners at the local level will be more intensely concerned and have a more comprehensive grasp of realities at the school site, which should put them in a better position to make appropriate decisions about the use of scarce resources. Decentralization is also based on the assumption that change is more likely to occur, and to occur more readily, if the emphasis is on local initiative rather than on reporting and hierarchy. Decentralization can be a way of freeing up partners at the school-site level to take more initiative to create effective responses to the educational needs of students.

There are three important ramifications of this set of assumptions:

1. *Reorientation of the Central Office Role.* The role must shift from one emphasizing regulating and initiating activities to one emphasizing facilitation, service, and responsiveness. Some current activities will continue to be dealt with best at the central level— for example, networking with other government agencies whose functions overlap with the school district; lobbying for resources at the district, state, and federal levels; and negotiating with teachers' unions. However, responsibilities for many other activities will shift to school sites. As responsibilities do gravitate to the school site, so will authority, requiring central office personnel to practice more restraint in their relationships with site personnel. Central office teaming also needs to be implemented as a model for schools, exhibiting less reliance on superintendent decision making and more on team decision making (Brown, 1991, p. 15).

2. *Reduction in the Number of Supervisory Personnel.* Decentralization, as noted, assumes less need for regulation and control so

fewer central office administrators should be required. If a school district's analysis of central office personnel needs supports this assumption, it should be possible to reallocate personnel to support the enlarged role to be played by school sites.

3. *Reduction in the Number of Administrative Layers in the School District.* The more direct the access, the better. With less need for regulation and increasing need for system responsiveness to local initiatives, the number of levels between the school board/superintendent level and the school-site level should be reduced. Given the professional nature of education, a flatter organizational structure is particularly appropriate. It should be feasible to establish and maintain a flatter structure because professionals need autonomy and the opportunity to take initiatives. Similarly, as a public trust, school districts should be accessible to direct influence by the communities they serve. The flatter the hierarchy, the more likely it is that this will happen.

Site-Based Management

Dismantling the regulatory role of the central office is not sufficient. Unless structural and role changes occur at the school site, the current strong initiatory role played by superintendents will probably just shift to the school principal. The partners at the school site must be challenged to define responsibilities and initiatives, to agree on who will be involved in the process, what roles they will play, and how accountability will be achieved.

Beyond changing decision-making structures, site-based management is intended to lead to better ways of to meeting the needs of students and the communities from which they come. The intent is to open a relatively closed system, so the partners can cooperatively explore delivery of education to meet site-identified goals. They "may plan staffing levels, employ or dismiss the principal, participate in the development of local curricula, and become involved in other important decisions affecting their schools" (Brown, 1991, p. 31). Some major changes will have to occur for this to become a reality:

1. *Efforts Must Be Made to Convince Potential Partners That Their Involvement and Participation Are Desired and Important.* This means students must be viewed as part of the system, parents and community as capable and concerned adults, and teachers and other staff members as interested and able to participate in management of the school. It will take considerable effort (see Chapter 4) to change behaviors and beliefs and provide the partners with the necessary skills required to work together cooperatively.

2. *Expectations Must Be Communicated Clearly by Central Office Leaders.* As the district decentralizes and plans are made to rebalance the system so more initiative can be taken at the school-site level, central office leaders must communicate their expectations very precisely. Doing business differently requires that the new "rules of the game" must be made clear and communicated a number of times and through different media. It is difficult enough to make major shifts in deeply ingrained and previously supported behaviors without also having to try to second-guess expectations.

3. *The Principal's Role Must Be Reconceptualized.* From being *the* authority figure at the top of the school pyramid, the principal must become the facilitator at the center of a complex web of partners. Principals must base their influence on "professional expertise and moral imperative rather than line authority. They must learn to lead by empowering rather than by controlling others" (Murphy, 1992, p. 125). Many principals will need help in making this role change. Some will see it as a challenge; others may be cautious but willing to try to change their leadership behaviors. Still others will feel threatened by these changing leadership behavior expectations.

4. *Teachers Must Share in Schoolwide Policy-Making and Be Involved in Implementation of Changes.* At present, schools are noted for a lack of opportunities for teachers and other personnel to come together to discuss and reach a consensus about mission, goals, curriculum content, or instructional delivery approaches. Restructuring will require a tilt away from the current black-and-white distinction of

administrator/teacher roles and the individualistic activities that typify schools today and toward shared leadership based on the cooperative activities that are being advocated in support of site-based management. Such changes are also logical given the increasing emphasis on cooperative learning being advocated for students. Adults in schools must role-model cooperation if they expect students to believe that it is important to behave this way.

5. *Structures That Encourage Involvement and Participation in Site-Based Management Must Be Created.* Some form of representative governance needs to be developed that assures continuance of a shared-management approach. This might take the form of school restructuring councils, advisory committees, school improvement teams, or other recognized structures. Explorations and agreements about such structures are more likely to come about if they are developed by the partners than if they are mandated by school boards or superintendents.

Widespread Involvement

All partners have something of value to offer to restructuring efforts. The payoffs of widespread involvement include the following:

1. Alternative perspectives and thus greater likelihood of new and different ideas being explored.
2. Increased chances of making advocates out of those who might remain critics if they are shut out of the process.
3. Potential to release positive energy and stimulate greater motivation to support and accomplish goals.
4. Increased likelihood of "ownership" of purposes and programs on the part of those who participate in the effort.
5. Opportunities for the partners to work with each other in ways that promote openness and trust.

Each of the partners has something special to offer to the process:

1. *School staffs*—including civil service personnel, non-class-room-based educators, teachers, and administrators—are most knowledgeable because they are intimately involved in the day-to-day workings of the school. They also have important and legitimate concerns that must be included in the discussion.

2. *Students* are coming to be viewed as "workers" rather than "consumers." Their participation gives them firsthand opportunities to practice critical thinking and to explore problem solving with adults. They also have a unique perspective that must be part of the dialog.

3. *Parents and other community members* have been closed out of the debate for too long. Their input is necessary, both because they have a legitimate role to play and because they must be recruited as partners who will work with the staff to enable students to achieve a meaningful education.

4. *Local business leaders* have a sensitivity about basic skills that are required in the economy. They also can partner with schools to identify and secure resources that are needed in support of the educational program.

Participative Decision Making

Because of the relative absence of precedents for participative decision making (PDM), relationships may be tenuous and unsettling until a common agenda is created, norms and rules are developed, and trust is established. It is one thing to declare that there will be PDM and quite another to institutionalize it. Problems likely to be encountered include the following:

1. Inclusion of role players (for example, school support staff members and community members) with little if any prior experience with or training in PDM, particularly as it relates to management of a school site.

2. Unrealistic expectations that teachers who are professionals who require autonomy and have operated individualistically will easily shift toward cooperative and collegial relationships.

3. Inability and/or unwillingness of principals to shed their authority rights and responsibilities and become facilitators and mediators.
4. Different experiences with PDM among members and general absence of skills related to PDM—problem solving, consensus building, team building, and maintenance skills—which takes more than goodwill and effort to implement.
5. Cries for efficiency, though often counterproductive to effectiveness, because PDM takes time and thus can be perceived as slowing progress.

These PDM issues can be dealt with, but the process requires purposeful and meaningful efforts. Care has to be given to the creation of supportive structures, to the enrichment of abilities through skill development, and to developing a clear sense of what issues should be submitted to PDM. The discussion must be limited to those issues that really belong to the partners as a group, both to assure that the task is not derailed and to protect specific role groups, such as teachers and administrators, who need to know that those things that should remain as their individual prerogatives will not be preempted.

In Closing

Recall the logical structure of this book: Purposes must be established first; then structural and role changes must be put in place to promote the purposes. However, even with directions and frameworks in place there is still need to enhance the ability of the partners to carry out their roles. In support of this aim, Chapter 4 focuses on beliefs and behaviors.

Promoting Supportive Beliefs and Behaviors

The results of restructuring are highly dependent on the *response-ability* of those who participate. Response-ability, or the extent to which participants are capable of conducting restructuring activities, is not something that can be assumed. Rather, it must be purposefully cultivated through strategies that focus on creating a commonality of beliefs and the willingness and ability to act on these beliefs through constructive behaviors. These strategies include learning from history, focusing on skill development, emphasizing teamwork and cooperation, promoting trust and risk taking, and building ownership among the partners in the endeavor.

Learning From History

Experience has taught educational leaders that certain things must be done during the early phases of restructuring:

1. *Define Terms*. The language employed in restructuring—decentralization, site-based management, accountability, and restructur-

ing itself—must be clarified. Similarly, the process that will take place and the outcomes that are desired need to be specified so participants can be clear about expectations.

2. *Define Roles.* Because of the major changes in roles that are likely to occur, efforts need to be made to clarify role changes for all participants. Modifications are likely in the roles of central office administrators and school-site administrators (as well as changes in role relationships between them), increasing expectations for teacher participation, more proactive student behaviors, and more central-important roles for parent and community participants.

3. *Manage Conflict.* Getting from current situations to more preferred states will require the ability to manage a lengthy transition, a time that will probably be marked by conflict. This transition time will call on all of your abilities to manage the conflicts that will arise.

4. *Invite Involvement.* Restructuring requires opening a relatively closed system and encouraging the partners to participate actively. Strong positive signals to this effect must be broadcast early and repeated often if meaningful involvement is going to emerge.

5. *Take an Incremental Approach.* A host of constraints must be overcome. These include school systems that reward compliance more than risk taking, schools that promote individualism and competition more than cooperation, and communities that are kept at arm's length more than they are invited to participate as equal partners with educators. Restructuring is a long-term activity because these deeply embedded realities require much time to change. Disillusionment is less likely if those involved understand this reality and are prepared to stay the course. "The total time frame from initiation to institutionalization is lengthy; even moderately complex changes take from three to five years, while major restructuring efforts can take five to ten years" (Fullan, 1991, p. 49).

Skill Development

The term *skill development* is used very purposefully, rather than an alternative such as *professional development*. *All* partners need to develop skills if the restructuring process is going to work. This is especially true of partners such as parents and students who have not previously been empowered and who have had little opportunity to learn the necessary skills to participate effectively. Purposeful efforts must be made to invite all partners to avail themselves of skill-development opportunities so they may be able to participate effectively and as equals in the restructuring process.

Two different kinds of skills must be developed:

1. *Governance Skills.* These skills are needed to participate in site-based management. They include mission and goal setting, planning, decision making, problem solving, conflict management, managing meetings, participating in teams, and assessing outcomes.

2. *Curriculum Development and Instructional Delivery.* Although teachers will continue to be the major participants in this activity, other partners will play an increasing role. Therefore, they need to have some knowledge of and ability in such activities as setting educational goals, developing and selecting curriculum content, identifying appropriate delivery approaches that promote such concepts as critical thinking and cooperative learning, and creating effective assessment tools.

The task of skill development may appear daunting given the extent of the issues and the number and diversity of participants involved. There is much that needs to be done to create meaningful skill-development experiences, but you are not starting from Day 1. Efforts to change schools over the past few decades have taught us about ways of providing necessary skills for governance as well as for curriculum development and instructional delivery. We know that skills are more likely to be learned and applied if 1) they are identified as necessary by those who will be learning them; 2) learners are involved in planning; and 3) learners include all partner groups and come from the same school site so lessons can be more readily transferred and applied to site-specific restructuring needs.

Where appropriate, individuals from the partner groups should be encouraged to provide leadership for skill development. For example, teachers who have effectively implemented critical thinking approaches in their classroom might be asked to run a workshop for teachers and perhaps for other partners at the school site. Site-based leadership for skill development is likely to be more focused on real needs than if it comes from central office personnel or outside consultants. It is also a way of promoting empowerment.

Finally, resources have to be reserved for this ongoing need (see Chapter 5). For example, resources will be needed for workshop/retreat sites, teacher substitutes, materials, materials development, and consultants. These resources will be needed for the long term, not just to get the process started, partly because as participants come and go new ones will need to be trained and partly because each phase of restructuring calls for different knowledge and skills.

Teamwork and Cooperation

Successful restructuring calls for cooperative participation, which is not usually promoted by school districts. In particular, students, parents, and other community members are frequently excluded from meaningful participation. For these partners to be convinced that they are really welcome as participants in the process, the system will have to send positive signals by actively conducting outreach activities such as organizing community meetings and seeking suggestions for restructuring.

Teachers are also peripheral players, partly because they are not frequently invited to engage in governance by administrators and partly because many of them narrowly define their role as one that focuses exclusively on the dynamics of the classroom rather than the overall school situation. Teachers will have to be convinced that their participation is desired and that their ideas will be taken seriously. Equally important, they need to be helped to change their role perceptions to include the important and legitimate role of schoolwide governance while being assured that their classroom-based professional prerogatives will not be jeopardized.

Effective teamwork and cooperation among the partners require skills such as good interpersonal and organizational communications, efficient and effective meetings behaviors, conflict management abilities, consensus decision making capabilities, and positive group maintenance behaviors. These are skills that can be learned, but developing effective teams takes time. It also calls for openness to change and willingness to take risks. Incentives may have to be created to promote positive responses to the development of cooperative teams. These might include mini-grants for team training at school sites willing to experiment with this process, promoting initiatives, and publicizing the good things that are going on at sites where partnering is being promoted.

Trust and Risk Taking

School restructuring is a transformational activity. It means changing what we do and how we do it, both of which require the willingness to take risks and to trust that partners will support each other. For most school districts this is not the current reality. Three things in particular have to be understood to move toward norms of trust and risk taking:

1. *Adopting New Things Means Letting Go of Old Things.* Changing global, national, and local environments call for changing educational emphases. However, many things are finite—for example, the length of the school day, the weeks in the school year, and the extent of information that can be absorbed by learners. This leads to the likelihood that some of what is now going on in schools will have to be modified, reduced, or done away with if other activities are going to be introduced. Limits of time and energy demand that we focus on that which is most important for learners.

2. *Standards for Restructuring Must Be Established and Expectations for Assessment Must Be Clarified.* Knowing the rules of the game

helps players feel more secure because they know what they are in for. It is easier to take risks if general guidelines for restructuring, such as expectations for mission and goal statements and establishment of a site-based partnership group, are provided. Similarly, if clear expectations for outcomes and how they will be measured are provided, those involved are not as likely to fear being held accountable for unrealistic results.

3. *Attitudes About Failure Must Be Changed.* Typically, teachers, schools, and communities have low tolerance for what they identify as "failure," whether it is students who perform poorly on norm-referenced tests, teachers who have poor discipline in their classrooms, or administrators who do not promote a positive climate in their schools.

These are failures that are not viewed as acceptable in times of stability and predictability. However, when times are unpredictable, we must take risks to make major changes in missions, goals, and activities. These are times of uncharted waters and, as such, are likely to lead to more so-called failures. However, mistakes are the stimulus for learning on which we create more effective responses. In fact, we should *celebrate failures* to encourage risk taking and analyze results to take advantage of the learning that accrues as a way of improving performance rather than hide the mistakes in shame. The likelihood and the value of making mistakes has to be recognized by all partners.

Ownership

Restructuring will ultimately prosper if *all* partners feel ownership—a sense that the effort is important and has the potential of meeting their own needs. They need to believe that they have much to gain from active participation. When *all* partners believe they can benefit, that win-win outcomes can be achieved, it is more likely that they will work together to accomplish goals. Competition will only be replaced by cooperation if partnering is viewed as mutually beneficial; creativity will be fostered when the partners are motivated to work together to identify purposes and to develop ways of achieving them.

Because of the importance of ownership, efforts should be made to promote this positive belief system. These efforts might include the following:

1. *Wide Involvement in Restructuring Activities* (see Chapter 3). As many partners as possible should be involved at every stage of the effort, including the identifying of mission and goals, the setting of standards for assessment of outcomes, and the developing of curriculum. Involvement can lead to learning: "Ownership of a reform cannot be achieved *in advance* [italics in original] of learning something new. A deep sense of ownership comes only through learning. In this sense, ownership is stronger in the middle of a successful change process than at the beginning and stronger still at the end. Ownership is both a process and a state" (Fullan & Miles, 1992, p. 749).

2. *Active Listening*. Only through listening can you hope to understand what others need, which is necessary if participants are going to act cooperatively and have a sense of ownership of outcomes. Judging, scolding, ignoring, pleading, intolerance, and threatening behaviors must be resisted. You need to resist judging others' words and try to understand their concerns.

Active listening skills that need to be taught and practiced include paraphrasing, describing behaviors, and sharing feelings. Active listening is more than passively hearing words. It is both hearing and responding, letting others know that you understand their meaning and appreciate their feelings, which are important foundations for the creation of trust and meaningful change.

3. *Regular Feedback About Restructuring Activities and Events*. Planners often become so absorbed in activities that they fail to consider the needs of others who will have to participate in the results of planning. Without access to information, those not directly involved in planning may grow uneasy and become suspicious of planners' motives or of what will be expected when they have to implement the plans. Rumors tend to spread like wildfire in such situations.

For these reasons, every effort should be made to keep all partners up-to-date on restructuring. Strategies include creating newsletters, making hot lines available, holding community meetings, putting on demonstrations, inviting interested parties to observe planning and implementation activities, and developing mechanisms such as suggestion boxes for individuals to initiate exchanges with planners.

4. *Sharing Outcomes.* The achievement of short-range and mid-range goals (see Chapter 2) should be publicized widely so motivation for continuing efforts will be enhanced. Accomplishments should be celebrated so that community building can be fostered and the partners can share perceptions of movement toward long-range goal achievement and can have opportunities to mark progress being made.

In Closing

Chapter 4 has explored the need to build a capacity among the partners for effective participation. This capacity, or response-ability—which must be present, or the best laid restructuring plans will not be implemented—is built through purposeful efforts to change beliefs and behaviors. These efforts will require application of resources. Chapter 5 examines the resources that must be identified and reserved to develop this capacity.

Providing Resources

There is a famous saying: "For want of a nail the shoe is lost, for want of a shoe the horse is lost, for want of a horse the rider is lost" (Hutchinson, 1945). This maxim gets to the point of why you need to think about resources for restructuring: for lack of money, motivated and capable people, adaptable space, and time to plan and do, even the best-laid restructuring plans will be lost. This chapter focuses on these four basic resource requirements.

Money

Although money alone cannot assure that restructuring will be successful, it is an essential energy base. Money is required for things such as these:

- Fees for consultants (insiders as well as outsiders), who need to be retained to develop participants' skills and provide advice about structures.
- Salaries for classroom substitutes for teachers involved in planning or implementation activities.
- Purchase of educational materials and compensation for those asked to develop site-based materials.

- Travel expenses for partners to visit school districts that are piloting important restructuring activities and to attend important local, regional, and national professional meetings.
- Compensation for involvement in ongoing and extensive planning and implementation activities.
- Funds for incentives (for example, mini-grants) that motivate appropriate behaviors and for dissemination of restructuring information to the partners.

It would be naive to assume that these things can be done without money. A recent survey, for example, found that it costs between $50,000 and $100,000 annually to keep significant change efforts moving in a single city high school (Louis & Miles, 1990).

You must make the effort to create a budget commitment for the kind of activities noted above. In most school districts, even 1% of the annual budget set aside for restructuring purposes can make an enormous difference. This may be difficult to do during recessionary times, but the precedent must be set. Even if new dollars are not available, you can undertake a review of the allocation of current resources. Hard decisions may have to be made to withhold some funds from specific budget lines to create the resource base to support the capacity for change.

The search for funds must take place at the school-district level, where school boards and superintendents can look for ways to rearrange the priorities of existing resources and to identify new funds. For example, you can seek grants from federal, state, and private sources, and you can petition the community for additional funds.

But the search for funds must also take place at the school-site level. If site-based budgeting is practiced, the partners can rearrange the priorities of resources as necessary and actively seek additional resources from nontraditional sources, such as the local business community, and through additional grant requests.

The bottom line is this: *Expecting major changes in purposes, structures, processes, and behaviors without providing the resources to get through the transition is not realistic.* The business world understands this reality more than the education world. Most large businesses have human resources departments, or some equivalent.

They know that they must spend resources to upgrade their employees' abilities to respond effectively to changing organizational and environmental situations. In fact, a good place to put energies toward education-business partnerships might be in the area of resource identification and acquisition, because there is so much sensitivity on the part of businesspeople to the need for resources. They can help identify probable needs, contribute and raise funds, and provide much expertise, usually gratis, to help with the effort.

People

Participants need "response-ability," as we discussed in the previous chapter. Two things in particular must exist among those who participate in the restructuring process:

1. *Goodwill and the Motivation to Make Schools Better.* People have to feel a real need if they are going to put a high enough priority on restructuring to become involved in the process. They also need to trust the motives of other participants and feel positive about working cooperatively to achieve purposes.

2. *The Ability to Participate in Governance and Educational Effectiveness Activities.* Goodwill is an important starting point, but it is not enough. Qualities for effective participation are also required. These include sufficient skills, knowledge about the intent of the effort, adequate information about the dynamics that are occurring, and the energy to stay the course.

Once the restructuring process is started, you must maintain the goodwill and the ability of those involved and continually seek to identify new partners who might be effective participants. For example, when positions open, hiring criteria should include evidence of the applicant's interest and ability to support restructuring activities that are underway. Further, appropriate partners should be involved in hiring decisions—for example, teachers and parents when a new principal is being selected. Similarly, if we expect students to believe us when we say that cooperative approaches to education are to be pursued in the classroom, we should model this approach by inviting them to work with the school's staff when curricular decisions are being made.

Each of the partner groups has legitimate and important contributions to make in restructuring. So you must take care to keep lines of communications open and to resolve conflicts as they occur. The effectiveness of restructuring is dependent on the goodwill and ability of the partners to work together.

Space

Most schools are physical reflections of a time when the United States was preoccupied with industrialization. Not surprisingly, schools came to look like the factories that their graduates filled. This situation sufficed while the "cult of efficiency" (Callahan, 1962) was the dominant paradigm.

We are moving away from an economy based exclusively on production, so this paradigm is no longer appropriate. Looking to the future, it is not at all clear what paradigm will dominate our thinking—but it is not likely to be the "cult of efficiency." We know that we are in a time of transition, and it is vital to experiment and explore alternative approaches to education.

Restructuring calls for flexibility in approaches to education that, in turn, calls for alternative spaces and flexible-use spaces, but most schools are composed of highly structured instructional spaces. Mostly, they are rectangular spaces, each with four walls built to accommodate one teacher and about 30 students.

You will have to become creative about modifying current spaces and constructing new spaces that promote flexibility in instructional approaches. We need spaces that hold several hundred students comfortably for mass presentations, and spaces for small group interaction and for one-on-one tutorials. Similarly, we need spaces that promote full inclusion of all groups of special-needs students and spaces that permit experimentation with schools-within-schools.

Beyond changing how you structure school-based spaces, you must also reconceptualize the notion of space in order to encompass the entire community. Some instruction may be better done in places such as business settings, government offices, the local market, or even in the nearby countryside. Cooperative relationships have to be developed so that these spaces can be made available to the schools. In return for using such spaces, you may have to become more receptive about opening your facilities for community uses.

The purposes of restructuring may be thwarted if you do not consider space needs. Current spaces have to be inventoried and thought must be given to ways of converting them into more flexible-use spaces. For example, if adjacent classrooms do not have weightbearing walls they can be modified into instructional pods with folding walls to encourage both small and large group instruction. Where current spaces cannot be altered they need to be included in replacement plans for construction, or new resources have to be identified to construct required spaces. Finally, you must scour the local community for appropriate spaces that can be attained gratis, by a trade-type arrangement, or through leasing to meet educational requirement needs.

Time

Time is your most finite and precious resource. Finding the time to bring the partners together to plan for restructuring, as well as to agree on changes in educational content and to implement alternative educational delivery systems, continues to be a major problem. Even when principals and teachers do make the commitment to give time to restructuring activities, usually they must take it from their regular school duties. One study found that when schools attempt changes, principals spend an average of 70 days a year and teachers spend 23 days a year on the efforts (Louis & Miles, 1990).

There is never enough time, particularly when so many partners are involved, each of whom has unique time constraints. Three time-related issues are particularly relevant:

1. *Community Members Are Not Available at the Same Time as School Personnel.* There are both more one-parent families and more

adults working now than ever before. This means there are fewer community members available during the working day when teachers and administrators can meet with them. As a result, to promote community access to the restructuring process, school personnel must be willing to meet with community members outside their workday—typically in the evening or on weekends. If administrators and teachers resist extending themselves in this way, the implicit message they send is that schools and communities are not really equal partners in the process.

2. *Teachers Lack Common Time to Come Together as a Group.* Schools are organized in ways that minimize opportunities for teachers to meet. Teaching is appropriately, but narrowly, defined as working with students in classrooms. Given this reality, as well as the belief that overseeing the school's activities is the administrator's job, it is not surprising that little attention has been given to making more time available for teachers to interact as a group.

Restructuring requires extensive teacher involvement in such activities as setting educational purposes, planning curriculum, designing appropriate instructional delivery systems, interviewing and selecting new personnel, providing professional feedback to colleagues, and creating assessment designs to monitor progress. It is also important to expand their role to include interacting with students, parents, and other community members in the determination of restructuring priorities.

Even within current structural constraints, there are options available to you that can bring teachers together in small groups and as total faculties. For example, you can do the following:

- Set aside staff development days.
- Reserve a portion of available substitute days.
- Add 10 or 15 minutes to the school day to accumulate early-release days.
- Encourage teachers to provide class coverage for each other.
- Use funds to pay teachers for meetings outside of school time.
- Plan for specialists to take over teachers' classes when there are restructuring meetings.

- Schedule common planning times for teachers who are on restructuring committees.
- Pay off-track teachers to meet when necessary if the district is involved with year-round education.

3. *Educational Innovations May Be Hampered by Existing Time Organization.* Implementation of innovative educational approaches may be blocked by the way schools organize instructional time. At the elementary level there are not as many constraints as at the secondary level. Still, the fact that most teachers work individually with a group of students does not promote teaming or more effective applications of teacher resources to meet students' educational needs. Nor does it provide a model for cooperative learning, which is what we expect of students.

The problem is more pervasive at the secondary level, where schools operate in ways that constrain educational change. For example, because curriculum is usually organized around disciplines, it is difficult to pursue content from multiple perspectives. Similarly, because instruction is delivered in defined time blocks that are typically limited to 50-minute periods, it is unrealistic to expect that in-depth, focused, and participative learning will occur. Students move along an imaginary conveyer belt, stopping off for brief periods at seven or eight specialized stations a day to collect their education credits. It is unlikely that this approach will encourage critical thinking, creative problem solving, or cooperative learning.

Creative time-block alternatives must be identified, and the way instructional time is blocked must be reexamined. For example, at both the elementary and secondary levels teaming can be encouraged by using more flexible instructional times that permit tutorials and small-group and large-group presentations. At the secondary level, more cross-department incentives can be provided to encourage movement toward a more holistic education based around ideas rather than disciplines. Similarly, schedules can be freed from the traditional Carnegie Unit approach so all school days do not look alike. For example, time can be organized into two-or-more-hour blocks so classes can meet two or three times a week instead of for 50 minutes every day of the week.

In Closing

Chapter 5 focuses on identifying and allocating scarce resources in ways that promote achievement of purposes. It brings us full circle in our look at the elements of restructuring. In the next three chapters, we will look at ways of making restructuring work. Chapter 6 examines what we have learned about the process of change and identifies strategies that can be employed to move toward institutionalization of restructuring changes. Chapter 7 identifies ways of assessing progress and presents tools to use to promote accountability. Finally, Chapter 8 presents exercises to use with partners as they work to achieve restructuring.

Changing Schools: Issues
and Strategies

S uccessful restructuring requires more than knowing where
you want to go—you must also know how you will get there.
This chapter explores the process of *managing the transition,* or getting from where you are to where you want to be. Managing the
transition is very different from managing continuity. Those leading restructuring efforts must understand this difference and have
the skills to conduct the activities that may be required. First, we
look at why it is so difficult to change schools. Second, we examine
some basic strategies that can improve the chances that changes
will persist long enough to embed them deeply in the culture of the
school organization.

Why Changing Schools Is So Difficult

Restructuring is the latest in a long parade of attempts to change
schools. However, as the Rand Corporation's studies of efforts to
change schools during the 1960s and the first half of the 1970s con-
cluded, there is precious little to show for the efforts that have been

made. Many innovations were adopted, some were successfully implemented, and fewer still have survived as long-run changes (Berman & McLaughlin, 1977).

Why is this the case? In large part it is because "the change process was not given sufficient attention" (SEDL, 1990, p. 1). Goodwill and good ideas are not sufficient. It also takes the skill to manage change:

> Serious education reform will never be achieved until there is a significant increase in the number of people—leaders and other participants alike—who have come to internalize and habitually act on basic knowledge of how successful change takes place (Fullan & Miles, 1992, p. 745).

The first thing would-be change managers need to understand is that difficulties can be expected, regardless of the specific change being promoted. Beyond your own lack of experience and knowledge about the change process, major difficulties include the following:

1. *Change Means Loss and Destabilization.* Whether related to current beliefs and ideologies or practices and behaviors, change requires letting go of something. Change dissolves meaning as new purposes and processes are explored and put in place. It also represents uncertainty and the likelihood of some discomfort. Change requires risk taking as participants gain new knowledge and learn new roles and skills, all demanding extra efforts and trust in the unknown.

Individuals who are having a difficult time with the destabilization that accompanies change are often labeled *resistant*, an oversimplified label that can be dysfunctional. Individuals' difficulties with change cannot be dealt with effectively unless they are "framed as natural responses to transition, not misunderstood as 'resistance' " (Fullan & Miles, 1992, p. 748).

2. *Change Is Confusing.* Enthusiasm dissipates quickly without clear purposes and strong support during the implementation process, and confusion can take its place. When you try something new,

you must define and communicate what you are doing. Further, it is one thing to declare a new direction, but quite another to make it happen, particularly without evidence of support from key players, such as resources, public endorsement, and waivers.

3. *Change Upsets Power Relationships.* Organizations are political systems. As such, shifts in the balance of power should be expected as a natural outcome of change, for reasons that have nothing to do with the content of the change itself. You must understand and manage power or else the power concerns that people have may negatively affect the outcomes of your change efforts. Those who have power based on status, roles, or control of resources may fear that they will lose their power. Similarly, those who do not have power may view the destabilization that accompanies change as an opportunity to gain it.

Strategies for Managing the Transition

Given the barriers that you probably will meet, you must manage the transition with the care you normally give to managing continuity. What strategies can help to enhance a successful transition?

1. *Shift Perspectives.* You must shift the emphasis from maintenance to change. The familiar saying "The only constant is change" is becoming ever more true for organizations that hope to persist in the coming decades. Because the world is changing so rapidly, we have little choice but to change how organizations function if we expect them to be relevant. This means the following changes must occur:

- You must be willing to let go of purposes and practices that may once have been appropriate but are no longer effective for the future. This requires the courage to upset the equilibrium intentionally, to "unfreeze" behaviors, to create the possibility of implementing desired changes. Movement is more likely after a period of purposeful disequilibrium. This can then be followed by institutionalization or, as Lewin refers to it, as "refreezing" the changes into the life of the organization (Lewin, 1964).

- You must consciously move from reactive to proactive behaviors. Schools tend to lag behind their environments, responding to shifting demands as best they can. During times of certainty this may suffice, but during times of uncertainty lagging behind is a sure path to purgatory! You must be more assertive, do more environmental scanning, and engage your community in ongoing dialogs—*as initiator, not responder*. You must raise important questions about purposes and practices and strive to keep schools and their environments in an effective partnership focusing on growth and improvement.
- You must accept that "failures" as a part of growth is to become the norm. Certainty and safety are not likely during times of major change. Rather, experimentation, mistakes, dead ends, re-experimentation, and learning by doing are likely to be the reality. You must understand this reality and be a champion and supporter of the pioneers who are willing to take the risks required for meaningful change to happen.
- Finally, schools must give up their addiction to piecemeal responses to complex problematic situations. Schools demand "quick fix" solutions, but complex problems are highly immune to these efforts. Leaders of change need to think in terms of overall, systemic change that includes focus on purposes, structures, behaviors, and outcomes. This requires comprehensive, broad-based thinking and the understanding that constant pressure must be kept up for many years for significant change to be institutionalized.

2. *Emphasize Continuity.* When efforts are made to shift perspectives in ways that encourage change-oriented behaviors, you must also promote a sense of security by emphasizing the knowns that will persist. These are not contradictory statements. Motivating change-oriented behaviors requires that those you are asking to change believe that life will be governed by constants more than by changes. For the following reasons, you must ensure a sense of sufficient stability:

- Participants need to feel secure. Most of us need a semblance of security. We are territorial by nature and need to be assured that continuity and regularity will be maintained, especially during times of change.
- The organization needs to maintain familiar points of reference to be able to define itself. This is necessary both as a way to foster daily, ongoing task focus and as a template on which to measure growth and change.

A realistic balance must be maintained, a balance that encourages participants to swim in the sea of change by reminding them that there will also be islands of continuity. Stability has to be available, even in the midst of change, so motivation does not turn into dysfunctional anxiety.

Even major school changes are likely to affect only a part of participants' lives. Why put all of the attention on this unsettling dynamic? If 20% of the situation is going to change, then a picture should be painted that reflects this reality. It does not make sense to create dysfunctional anxiety by putting 80% of the focus on the change effort.

3. *Focus on the School Organization's Culture.* All organizations develop their own distinctive cultures. A culture is composed of "the *norms* that inform people what is acceptable and what is not, the dominant *values* that the organization cherishes above others, [and] the *basic assumptions and beliefs* that are shared by members" (Owens, 1991, p. 28) [italics in original]. Some cultures promote conformity and security whereas others encourage growth and risk taking.

Unfortunately for those attempting to introduce major changes, schools typically approximate the conforming/security type of culture. In fact, they exhibit a remarkable tenacity, remaining relatively consistent across time and space. Thus it may take considerable effort, but nothing short of a major shift of the school's culture toward growth and risk taking will lead to institutionalization of change. Leadership behaviors in support of this objective include the following:

- Establishing a clear organizational mission that has been thoughtfully developed as a result of extensive interaction among the partners.
- Keeping all participants aware of the mission and emphasizing that it is more than mere words—it is what all actions are based on.
- Consciously reflecting and promoting the kind of culture that is desired. Such a culture must include high trust, taking risks, seeking and sharing information, promoting involvement, and ownership (Stewart, 1986).

4. *Provide Leadership for Change.* Change management is an important leadership act, requiring the ability to shape and communicate the assumptions and values that are at the core of the desired changes (Schein, 1986). This, in turn, requires that leaders do the following:

- Pay attention to the purposes being espoused.
- Role model for others by pursuing these purposes.
- Send important signals by supporting and rewarding those who are willing to initiate purpose-related activities.
- Recruit partners who can help achieve accepted purposes.

Ultimately, if change is going to be implemented leadership must be viewed as a function, not a person. That is, all partners must pay attention to the four leadership roles identified above. If this is achieved, the desired culture very likely will be deeply embedded and form a powerful and positive foundation for effective change.

5. *Provide Skill Development.* Supporting ongoing learning, as noted in Chapter 4, is important to promote enthusiasm, build confidence, and create a "can do" attitude. This includes coaching participants as they encounter new situations, honoring "failures" or mistakes, and providing help so participants become more confident and effective in their governance and educational change efforts. Different thinking is required, thinking that moves in the following directions:

- Away from centrally defined skill-development-package activities and toward locally generated needs assessments and decision making that drive skill development efforts.
- Away from skill development efforts driven by "experts" (that is, external consultants and/or central office personnel) and toward experiences planned by participants and involving them as leaders in the delivery of skill development sessions.
- Away from skill development limited to teachers and toward inclusion of *all* participants in the effort.
- Away from skill development offered at central locations that include participants from various sites and toward activities taking place at a school site that is pursuing restructuring and is limited to partners from that site.
- Away from one-shot efforts and toward sustained growth opportunities with resources provided for necessary materials and supplies as well as for follow-up efforts.

6. *Monitor the Process.* Yardsticks that measure progress toward change are needed to promote enthusiasm and ongoing commitment. This is accomplished by setting clear expectations and assessing movement or developing meaningful standards and evaluating outcomes. Without attention to this measurement process, which is explored more fully in Chapter 7, participants have no way of knowing the extent to which they are achieving purposes.

In Closing

Change disrupts organizational routines—doing things the first time is very different from doing them the hundredth time. First-time activities call for effective transition management. If we become fixated on intended future states, we will not focus on successfully managing the transition, which is so important if we expect to get to that future state. Navigating transitions effectively requires the following:

- Partners must coalesce around purposes.

- Necessary organizational capacities must be developed—
  for example, change-oriented roles are created, change
  managers are found who have the status to get things done,
  resources are reserved for promotion of the change, flexible
  plans are agreed on to guide the effort, and structures are
  created for widespread involvement and experimentation.
- Assessment processes that promote "knowing" what is
  happening and what progress is/is not being made must be
  developed.

Managing the transition is an important activity, one that is often
minimized or overlooked in restructuring efforts. As the leader of
the restructuring efforts, you are strongly encouraged to seek more
knowledge about organizational change and gain the necessary
skills to conduct this activity. The remaining restructuring activity
that must be considered is how to assess the process. This important topic is explored in Chapter 7.

Assessing Restructuring Efforts

The concern about assessment is, in part, the result of political realities. Resource givers, demanding value for dollars granted, are asking "Are we getting our monies' worth?" (Bailey, 1992, p. 108). However, assessment can and should be an activity that does more than assure satisfaction for resource givers. Those engaged in restructuring also need to have assessment information to keep the process on target.

Assessment is not a new concept—good managers and good teachers have always practiced it. In the past, though, assessment was hit-and-miss and somewhat limited in scope:

> Under centralization, assessment on how schools are performing is often infrequent . . . few indicators are normally provided to show the various levels of program success or failure. And only rarely is some statement made to show the extent to which students and parents are satisfied with the service provided them (Brown, 1991, p. 27).

What *is* new is the intensity of interest about assessment and the challenge to begin these efforts at the school-site level. This chapter covers five assessment-related topics: purposes, guidelines, leadership activities, methods, and reporting results.

Purposes of Assessment

We can distinguish three purposes of assessment. First, assessment helps us "set standards, create instruction pathways, motivate performance, provide diagnostic feedback, assess/evaluate progress, and communicate progress to others" (Herman, Aschbacher, & Winters, 1992, p. 2). The wider the involvement and the more partners included in restructuring, the more important it becomes to communicate progress. If progress is communicated clearly, such information can provide "the basis for identifying staff development or materials needs, and for targeting and assessing plans for improvement" (Herman et al., 1992, p. 3).

Second, site-based management is changing the way we do business in education, and there is need for accountability and thus for assessment. Authority and responsibility are devolving to the school site. The partners at the school-site level are establishing policy and deciding about mission and goals, budgeting, personnel selection and retention, curricular content, and instructional delivery systems. Whereas "school personnel in centralized districts do not feel particularly accountable to anyone" (Brown, 1991, p. 27), with the greater level of freedom to initiate and decide that exists when site-based management is practiced comes an obligation to be held accountable for results.

Third, assessment serves the important purpose of reminding participants of the cyclical nature of education. We learn from our efforts, whether mistakes or breakthroughs. Because every year represents another opportunity to serve students better, assessment feedback can be applied to improve restructuring efforts. In short, assessment outcomes have the potential of guiding future efforts as well as of establishing results of past efforts.

Guidelines for Assessment

At least eight guidelines should be considered in planning the assessment effort:

1. *It Should Be Purpose-Driven.* Chapter 2, which focuses on purpose setting, encourages those guiding restructuring efforts to develop long-term, mid-range, and short-term goals. If these goals are established, the base for assessment is already in place. The assessment effort is aimed at establishing the extent to which these goals are being achieved and at making changes in strategies where information indicates it is necessary.

2. *It Should Include Focus on Both Governance and Education.* Structural and role modifications are governance changes aimed at improving relationships and increasing cooperation among the partners. The extent to which these are agreed on and take effect must be established in order to know whether restructuring governance efforts are functioning well. Educational improvement is the intended outcome of restructuring. The extent to which this is actually occurring is important to know so future efforts can be designed effectively.

3. *It Should Test Things That Matter to the Partners.* Assessing lets people know "what's important, what deserves focus, and what we expect as good performance. In the process, significant stakes are often associated with test results—classroom grades, college admission decisions, job security, self-satisfaction, and other perks— thus motivating performance" (Herman et al., 1992, p. 3).

4. *It Should Emphasize Local Outcomes-Based Initiatives.* The idea is to ascertain the extent to which outcomes that matter, given established purposes, are being pursued. This will more likely be the case if assessment instruments are locally designed. For example, regarding education improvement, it is difficult for norm-referenced tests (for example, the Iowa Test) to get at things that matter, such as attitudes about cooperative learning or the ability to think critically or solve complex problems. When those who create purposes and plan implementation activities are involved in developing assessment strategies and instruments, the focus is more likely to be used to guide future efforts.

5. *It Should Serve the Effort, But Not Cause Undue Anxiety*. Restructuring is more likely to be served without unnecessary anxiety if the following are true:

- The assessment process is an integral part of restructuring and is used as a tool to enhance motivation rather than to create fear and apprehension: "If the scrutiny is too precise, the empowerment tone can be minimized to the point of being ineffective" (Bailey, 1992, p. 112).
- The process emphasizes growth and development rather than causing teachers to "teach to the test" or governance groups to second-guess preferences of superintendents and school boards.
- The process is aimed at creating rich and meaningful information rather than emphasizing counting, especially for counting's sake. Impressions of important outcomes are more important than statistically significant tests of insignificant outcomes! Reputedly, Albert Einstein had a statement posted on his office wall: "Not everything that counts can be counted and not everything that can be counted counts" (Herman et al., 1992, p. v).

6. *It Should Make Multiple Use of Information*. Using information that has already been developed for other purposes but can also serve assessment purposes is participant-friendly. Imposing extensive expectations for assessment on participants who may already be overcommitted can have a negative effect on enthusiasm and continued participation. Existing information, such as restructuring council minutes, climate surveys, and teacher-created educational outcomes tests, can be used to provide important information without overburdening the participants.

7. *It Should Employ Multiple Indicators to Establish Outcomes*. Single indicators are not likely to establish progress toward the achievement of complex outcomes as fully as multiple indicators (for example, observations, interviews, and test results). "Multiple indicators as determined at the local site come much closer to explaining the complex social phenomenon of schooling" (Bailey, 1992, p. 127).

8. *It Should Include Information About All Phases of the Effort.* Figure 7.1 offers a way of organizing thinking along three phases of the assessment effort:

- *Purpose/standard setting:* Mission and goals that are agreed on by the participants should set the expectations to be measured. They must be understood and widely shared if they are to serve as the template for the entire effort.
- *Monitoring progress:* The extent to which processes that have been established are leading to hoped-for results can be tested by *formative evaluation.* It can help establish what particular stage of development the effort has achieved—no change, awareness raising, experimentation with alternative purposes or processes, implementation, and institutionalization. The point is to monitor the system on a regular basis so needed modifications can be taken to keep the system on course.
- *Assessing outcomes:* Whether goals are actually being achieved can be established by *summative evaluation,* which is effective for short-range, mid-range, and long-range goals.

Those involved in developing accountability strategies can use Figure 7.1 to brainstorm activities that should be conducted in each of the three phases, for both governance and educational improvement. Such a discussion would help assure a holistic approach to the accountability of efforts.

Leadership Activities for Assessment

Regularized and meaningful assessment requires that you take an active part in the process. In particular, superintendents and their support staffs must provide clear statements of purposes for assessment, establish the basic ground rules of the process to be followed, specify expectations for information to be provided, and help participants acquire the skill and knowledge required. Finally, if outside expertise is needed to assure that effective approaches are developed, you must set aside resources for this purpose.

Stages	Governance Activities	Educational Activities
Setting Purposes/Standards		
Monitoring Progress		
Assessing Outcomes		

Figure 7.1. A framework to guide assessment activities.

Principals must work with participants at the school site to focus the effort on agreed-on purposes, to facilitate the work flow, to maintain motivation, and to assure sufficient time and personnel to conduct the effort. Many principals will need intensive training before they can conduct these activities with confidence. Many will also have to become more adept at working with other partners, particularly teachers, to identify meaningful assessment activities.

Methods for Assessment

There is not sufficient space, nor is it the purpose of this chapter, to provide a full exposition of assessment methodology (for greater depth, see Conway, Jennings, & Milstein, 1974). Briefly, however, those charged with conducting assessments—whether of governance activities or educational activities and other than norm-referenced academic tests or comparable instruments that test such things as school climate—will likely use some combination of the following:

- *Interviews*
  Advantages: Easy to design; potential for much information; flexible use; can build trust.
  Disadvantages: Difficult to quantify results; take much time to do; open to interviewer bias.
- *Questionnaires*
  Advantages: Easy to quantify; much output for little effort; can be objective.
  Disadvantages: Take much time to prepare; not flexible or able to pursue information in depth.
- *Observations*
  Advantages: Depth of information obtained.
  Disadvantages: Open to bias in recording and analyzing information; take much time to do.
- *Records and Documents*
  Advantages: Easy to design and control the process; efficient use of time.
  Disadvantages: Documents may not have necessary depth of information (public versus real data).

Reporting the Results

Reporting the results brings the assessment process full circle. This final stage of the effort keeps the partners apprised of real progress toward agreed-on purposes and provides a basis for further deliberation and decision making aimed at keeping the restructuring effort on track.

Some feedback may be done through one-way communication if the aim is solely to inform interested parties of assessment results. However, if the assessment is going to have an impact on restructuring, efforts must be made to engage the participants in a conversation. This process, which is often referred to as *survey-feedback* (see Bowers & Franklin, 1974), if done well can offer the following:

- Provide a coherent and shared snapshot concerning current realities.
- Identify important issues that need to be addressed.
- Lead to clarity about next steps and future directions.
- Motivate the partners to continue their efforts.

In short, survey-feedback can assess the past and the current situation and guide future developments. For these objectives to be achieved, you must provide these three ongoing requirements:

1. *Organize Information So It Can Be Understood.* The information must be digested, condensed, and prepared for feedback. The intent should be to provide information that is organized in ways that participants can understand the extent to which purposes are being achieved. Given the diversity of the participants, take care to avoid jargon or leave any members at a disadvantage in participating in the review of assessment information.

2. *Facilitate the Dialog.* Those receiving feedback may be school board members, central office personnel, site-based educators, students, parents, or other community members, or some combination of these participants. Knowing the composition of the group is the first step in matching the tenor of the feedback to the needs, knowledge, and interests of those involved. The second step is to guide participants effectively through the information feedback to be sure that it is understood. The third step is to encourage them to explore how the information can provide insights about the achievement of agreed-on purposes. The final step is to facilitate group discussion of the conclusions and decisions about next steps to take as a result of the examination of assessment information.

3. *Keep the Process Moving.* Assessment and feedback are not one-shot efforts. For example, the information obtained may lead to a series of meetings, sometimes with only one or a few of the partner groups (for example, a briefing for the school board or a review by the central office staff and school principals) and at other times with all partners in public forums. These discussions can keep participants informed and enthusiastic about restructuring.

In Closing

The next cycle of activities begins with the assessment of past results, which should serve as the baseline on which to measure future progress. Therefore, the information obtained should not be left to gather dust in a file drawer. It must be accessible and you must remind partners of its existence and importance.

Assessment and accountability are here to stay. The public's insistence on it as well as the shift from centralized authority to school-based, participative management will lead to further emphasis on documentation of restructuring efforts and outcomes. Assessment can be a powerful vehicle in support of restructuring efforts if it is understood and used in effective ways. Assessment processes advocated to insure accountability may be viewed as novel today, but they will become part of the fabric of the system in the future.

Chapter 8 completes the exploration of restructuring by suggesting a number of activities that can be helpful in facilitating the process.

Activities to Promote
Restructuring

Tell me, I forget
Show me, I remember
Involve me, I understand

This ancient Chinese proverb underscores the point that the success of restructuring efforts depends on getting participants actively involved in the process. If they are going to understand, you must become familiar with ways of promoting active and positive involvement.

I offer a variety of activities in this final chapter that can help you with this task, under the following categories—identifying starting points and setting expectations; promoting cooperation and teaming; stimulating creativity; rewarding efforts; solving problems; and making decisions. If you find the activities helpful, use the references provided as well as other resources at your disposal to build a larger repertoire to help energize restructuring efforts.

Identifying Starting Points and Setting Expectations

These activities can help stimulate the discussion, establish agreements about priority needs, and set basic rules to guide the effort.

Elements in Restructuring. Use Figure 1.1 to establish a baseline for restructuring activities. After the four quadrants and the elements within them are defined, the group can examine them and identify *strengths* (what is already being done well) and *weaknesses* (what is not now being done or not being done effectively). Agreements can be recorded and become the basis for arranging priorities of the activities to be pursued.

Culture/Climate/Satisfaction Surveys. It is important to establish how conducive the current school environment is to cooperation, risk taking, trust, and growth. If it is not very conducive, you must improve the situation so restructuring can take root. There are instruments that test culture, climate, and satisfaction (for example, Shaheen & Roberts, 1974; National Association of Secondary Principals, 1986), but you may want to consider developing your own instruments. Besides specifically pinpointing areas of interest, home-grown instrument creation supports the development of cooperation among the partners who plan and conduct activities.

What's Excellent, OK, Not Being Done? This activity identifies current strengths and necessary changes. It also assures participants there will be continuity in the midst of change and some things will be held safe. First, ask participants to identify what is excellent about their school and should be protected. Once agreements are identified, ask them to identify what is OK about their school but can be better if they are willing to change things. Finally, ask the group to identify what needs to be done that is not happening now or could be more effective. The second and third questions can lead to a beginning plan for action, but the questions need to be asked in the order suggested so an atmosphere of security and safety is established before participants are asked to risk identifying deficits.

Yours/Mine/Ours. This activity, which is intended to clarify which areas are legitimate topics for group exploration and which should be reserved for particular role groups, can be helpful in two ways. First, it establishes parameters—what are and what are not the group's prerogatives? This helps to delimit the agenda and keep the group on track. Second, it assures specific partners, such as administrators and teachers, that activities that legitimately belong to them will remain under their control. Give the participants a set of note cards—one for the total group and one for each of the role groups involved—and ask them to write what activities should be conducted by the role group on each card as well as those that should be conducted by the entire group. Then sort the cards by role groups and the entire group. Review the responses with the group and have participants discuss the outcomes. Agreements are recorded and disseminated (for more detail, see Milstein, 1993).

Promoting Cooperation and Teaming

These activities are aimed at creating effective working environments among participants.

Norming. Agreement about norms—such as openness, accepting constructive criticism, empathy, follow-through on commitments, respect, and being on time—can help establish a positive working environment. New groups can benefit from some discussion and agreement about norms. Members can suggest norms and the group can agree on those it expects members to support. These norms can be put in writing, reviewed periodically, and shared with participants who join the group at a later time.

Cooperation, Competition, and Individualization. Teaching is most frequently performed in isolation. In fact, rather than cooperate, teachers are more likely to compete for scarce resources such as materials and preferred schedules. Similarly, communities and schools often view each other as adversaries rather than as partners. It can be helpful to engage participants in an exercise that clarifies current realities and identifies future preferences. This can emphasize the need to change from a culture that promotes individual efforts and inappropriate competition to one that supports cooperation in restructuring efforts. After terms are defined, ask the participants to estimate the percentage of time that they are now engaged in cooperative, competitive, and individualized activities and to provide examples for each. After the results are discussed, ask the participants to place percentages on these three dynamics as they prefer them to be. After discussion again, plans can be made to move toward preferred states (for more details about the concepts, see Johnson & Johnson, 1991, p. 87).

Team Stages. It takes time to develop effective teams. They go through several distinct stages: *forming* (common tasks are recognized), *storming* (leadership and control issues arise), *norming* (agreements about norms, rules, and policies are developed), and *performing* (tasks are accomplished) (Fay & Doyle, 1982; Tuckman, 1965). After these stages are described and defined, have the participants discuss this evolution, agree on where their team is currently, and identify activities that can help the team continue its development.

Team Tasks and Team Maintenance (Harris, 1985; Schmuck & Runkel, 1985). An effective team gets the job done. Members take on such roles such as shaping ideas, pursuing and completing tasks, identifying resources, and evaluating results. An effective team also remains cohesive by focusing on such maintenance activities as encouraging, active listening, checking for involvement, managing conflicts, and developing trust. Both sets of activities must exist if the team is to remain effective over time. Periodic reviews by the team can identify whether these roles are being performed and, if so, by whom. Where deficits are identified the team can explore options for change.

Stimulating Creativity

I suggested earlier that if you do what you have always done you will get what you have always gotten. Different ways of interacting need to be encouraged to avoid falling into old thinking patterns.

Buzz Groups. All participants should be involved as thinkers as well as doers to increase the likelihood of important ideas surfacing and to increase the likelihood of members understanding and being committed to the group's decisions. When groups are large it is difficult for this to happen, so it can be helpful to create temporary smaller groups whenever wide participation is desired. Asking people to meet in "buzz groups" of four to eight members can promote this. Requests for buzz groups can be made by the leader or by group members, and they can be used for a few minutes or for longer periods, depending on the situation.

Pyramiding. This is another way of promoting wide involvement. Initially, ask each member to write out two or three suggestions about the topic being explored. Then, have members meet in groups of three or four to share their ideas and identify those they can support. Next, have two groups join to identify things they agree on across their lists. Depending on the size of the total group, this process might be repeated, bringing more groups together. Ultimately there should be a sharing and agreeing session of the total group.

Brainstorming. This activity is aimed at encouraging the development of creative solutions to problems. During the first stage, ask members to suggest ways of responding to a problem, regardless of how impractical they might appear to be. Ground rules during this stage include 1) record all ideas, 2) no criticism, 3) no attempts to modify ideas, and 4) tolerance of silences—a fertile time of discovery when people are probably thinking! During the second stage, have the group review and modify the list of ideas that has been generated. Some ideas may be modified, some may be combined, and some may be dropped. During the third stage, if results justify it, decisions can be made.

Rewarding Efforts

Individuals and schools need to be recognized for their efforts. Recognition affects satisfaction, motivation, and risk taking positively.

Recognition. Besides rewarding participants, recognition can further restructuring by enhancing motivation. It can come in many forms. District newsletters can highlight progress made by individuals, teams, schools, or the entire district. Participants can receive plaques or other lasting forms of recognition for their contributions. Teachers can be asked to do demonstrations of classroom activities they have developed that are working well. Participants with special skills can be asked to plan for and conduct workshops. You can develop other strategies for recognition locally.

Mini-Grants. Resources can be reserved to promote creativity. It does not take extensive funding to encourage the development and implementation of locally generated ideas. Mini-grants make it possible to promote experimentation, bypassing extensive approval processes. These grants can be made to individuals, groups, or an entire school community.

Share Fairs. Opportunities can be provided for participants to share what they are doing to improve governance and educational outcomes. Share fairs can be organized within a school, across a school district, or even across neighboring school districts. They can include booths with artifacts on display, demonstration sessions with opportunities for questions and answers, and keynote addresses by noted authorities whose participation may both enhance recognition and suggest further activities to be considered.

Solving Problems

Restructuring is a systemic approach to school change. Because it requires dealing with a comprehensive set of governance and educational dynamics, those involved can easily become over-whelmed by complex problems.

Force-Field Analysis. This technique, initially developed by Kurt Lewin (1951; for further details see Schmuck & Runkel, 1985, pp. 222-224), requires the group to clarify a problem first, translate it into a goal to be achieved, and then identify the existing "forces" that facilitate and hinder achievement of the goal. Finally, the group will develop strategies to alter the balance of these forces. The exercise encourages participants to think about goals rather than current problems; breaks problems down into smaller, more manageable pieces; and focuses efforts on those elements that are most amenable to change.

Situation, Target, Path (STP). This exercise, developed by Schmuck and Runkel (1985; for a full description, see pp. 216-222), can help a group clarify the nature of problems. The issue(s) can reside in any of three places—beliefs about the present situation (*S*), the goal or target (*T*), or the actions or path (*P*) to be used to get from the current situation to the goal. STP sessions can be used to help the group share perceptions and identify where to place its energies.

Making Decisions

Moving from a hierarchical system that limits participation to a decentralized system that invites new partners to become in-volved in the process can easily lead to conflicts about how decisions are going to be made. What does participation mean? Who has what prerogatives? What issues should be open to wider involvement in decision making?

Leadership and Decision Making. Agreement about the roles of group leaders and members in decision making can help avoid potential conflicts and misunderstandings. Tannenbaum and Schmidt (1958) present a continuum of possibilities ranging from the leader 1) deciding and announcing decisions; 2) selling decisions to the group; 3) announcing decisions and permitting questions; 4) presenting tentative decisions, consulting with the group, and then deciding; 5) presenting problems, asking for ideas, and then deciding; 6) presenting problem and boundaries and the group deciding; to 7) giving the group freedom to define problems and decide. You can present these options to participants to explore so limits can be agreed on and norms can be established.

Decision-Making Roles. This exercise focuses on helping partners negotiate agreements about roles each should play when making decisions about various issues (Schmuck & Runkel, 1985, p. 292). Develop a matrix that includes all role groups (for example, administrators, teachers, parents, students) as columns and the issue areas anticipated as requiring deliberation and decision making (for example, goals, budgets, materials, schedules) as rows. Then define decision role options—give information, be informed, be consulted, participate in making the decision, veto power, final authority. Finally, have the group share perceptions about issue areas and seek to come to agreements about appropriate decision-making prerogatives for different role players.

Routine/Evolutionary/Revolutionary Decisions Continuum. Groups must be involved when information is shared, and agreements need to be developed before key decisions are made. Recognizing that some decisions are best left to individuals and others require group participation is an important foundation for effective restructuring. *Routine decisions* are those about which there is wide agreement. *Evolutionary decisions* are those about which there has been some group exploration but that may, at key points in time, call for further group deliberation. *Revolutionary decisions* are those related to new goals, policies, and procedures. It is not efficient or effective to put routine decisions or many evolutionary decisions before the total group. Describing the continuum to the group can lead them to clarify and agree on what should and should not be the focus of their attention.

Consensus Decision Making. Decisions can be made by individuals, small groups, majority vote, or by consensus. When decisions need to be made cooperatively by the partners, you should pursue consensus decision making because the decision is more likely to be creative and result in a high degree of commitment. Consensus decision making is not widely pursued because it is not efficient, taking much time and skill. However, decision making by majority vote is likely to result in a minority that is opposed to the decision that is made. Consensus does not mean that all group members agree about a decision, but it does mean that every member 1) understands the issues at hand; 2) has a chance to describe how he or she feels about issues and the possible responses being explored; and 3) is willing to publicly go along with the group's preferred solution, even though it may not be his or her choice. Helping the group understand the meaning of consensus and the importance of practicing it when appropriate can do much to maintain goodwill, cooperation, and trust, and to enhance the quality of the decisions that are made.

In Closing

We can expect that restructuring will become a way of life in schools as a result of the escalating changes we are witnessing in the United States and, for that matter, across the world. The activities I present in this chapter can help motivate effective restructuring. We know too well how important it is that these efforts succeed. We are at a crossroads in public education, a choice point that will impact the future of our students and our country for decades to come. Only the best efforts to restructure will suffice.

Annotated Bibliography and References

Annotated Bibliography

I have assembled the following selected annotations for those readers who would like to explore restructuring-related topics in more detail.

Bailey, W. J. (1992). *Power to the schools*. Newbury Park, CA: Corwin Press.

Written by a former superintendent, this book includes an examination of the context that has stimulated restructuring as well as practical guidelines for initiating restructuring activities. Emphasis is placed on meaningful involvement of school faculties, ways of improving student learning, and initiating and monitoring changes.

Brown, D. J. (1991). *Decentralization*. Newbury Park, CA: Corwin Press.

This book enumerates the possibilities and pitfalls associated with school district restructuring. Site-based management, the intended outcome and opposite side of the coin of centralization, is examined. It also provides practical guidelines for the development of district policies regarding allocation, budgeting, and accountability.

Fiske, E. B. (1992). *Smart schools, smart kids.* New York: Touchstone Books.

This book ranges across the educational landscape to find examples of schools that work and explores the thinking behind these lighthouse settings. Focusing on educational programs, it provides readers with valuable insights that might help them improve their own schools. The book includes a "Resource Guide to Smart Schools."

Fullan, M. G. (1991). *The meaning of educational change* (2nd ed.). New York: Teachers College Press.

This seminal book provides a solid foundation for understanding change and innovation in education. Included are causes, planning, and processes. Particular emphases are placed on teachers, principals, students, district administrators, consultants, and communities.

Herman, J. L., Aschbacher, P. R., & Winters, L. (1992). *A practical guide to alternative assessment.* Alexandria, VA: Association for Supervision and Curriculum Development.

This guide to effective assessment, which is written in practitioner language, encourages readers to focus on things that are important rather than things that can be counted. It also encourages readers to create their own assessment tools rather than rely on standardized instruments that may not be appropriate for their particular needs. It provides specific ideas for instrument development.

Johnson, D. W., & Johnson, F. P. (1991). *Joining together* (4th ed.). Englewood Cliffs, NJ: Prentice Hall.

This work explores various aspects of developing and maintaining effective groups, including goal setting, communications, leadership, decision making, conflict, and team development. It presents concepts as well as exercises for group development efforts.

Murphy, J. (1991). *Restructuring schools.* New York: Teachers College Press.

Includes a background and definition of restructuring, as well as a useful categorization of the various elements that should be considered. Emphasis is given to the "core technology" of curriculum and instruction. A realistic perspective is encouraged regarding implementation issues and realities.

National LEADership Network Study Group on Restructuring Schools (1991). *Developing leaders for restructuring schools.* Washington, DC: U.S. Department of Education.

A group composed of LEAD directors from nine states and others examines the education and training that school leaders require to be able to guide restructuring. Based on feedback from administrators involved in restructuring, the report emphasizes leadership development and changing leadership role expectations.

Schmuck, R. A., & Runkel, P. J. (1985). *The handbook of organization development in schools* (3rd ed.). Prospect Heights, IL: Waveland Press.

Restructuring ultimately is dependent on schools' capacities for change and renewal. This book introduces the technology of organization development and presents in practical terms techniques for conducting such activities as diagnosis, survey-feedback, intervention, and evaluation. In addition, it examines goal setting, communications, problem solving, decision making, and other group effectiveness concerns and suggests activities for improvement.

References

Bailey, W. J. (1992). *Power to the schools.* Newbury Park, CA: Corwin Press.

Berman, P., & McLaughlin, M. (1977). *Federal programs supporting educational change: Vol. 7. Factors affecting implementation and continuation.* Santa Monica, CA: Rand Corporation.

Bowers, D. G., & Franklin, J. L. (1974). Basic concepts of survey feedback. *The 1974 annual handbook for group facilitators.* San Diego, CA: University Associates Publishers.

Brown, D. J. (1991). *Decentralization.* Newbury Park, CA: Corwin Press.

Caldwell, B. J., & Spinks, J. M. (1992). *Leading the self-managing school.* London: The Falmer Press.

Callahan, R. E. (1962). *Education and the cult of efficiency*. Chicago: University of Chicago Press.

Carnegie Forum on Education and the Economy. (1986). *A nation prepared: Teachers for the 21st century*. Washington, DC: Author.

Center on Organization and Restructuring of Schools. (1992, Fall). Estimating the extent of school restructuring. *Brief, 4,* 1-4.

Chin, R., & Benne, K. D. (1969). General strategies for effecting change. In W. G. Bennis, K. D. Benne, & R. Chin (Eds.). *Planning of change* (2nd. ed.). New York: Holt, Rinehart & Winston.

Conway, J. A., Jennings, R. E., & Milstein, M. M. (1974). *Understanding communities*. Englewood Cliffs, NJ: Prentice Hall.

Fay, P. P., & Doyle, A. G. (1982). Stages of group development. *The 1982 annual for facilitators, trainers, and consultants*. San Diego, CA: University Associates.

Fullan, M. G. (1991). *The meaning of educational change*. New York: Teachers College Press.

Fullan, M. G., & Miles, M. B. (1992). Getting reform right: What works and what doesn't. *Phi Delta Kappan, 73*(10), 745-752.

Hall, G. E., & Hord, S. M. (1987). *Change in schools*. Albany, NY: State University of New York Press.

Harris, P. R. (1985). *Management in transition*. San Francisco: Jossey-Bass.

Herman, J. L., Aschbacher, P. R., & Winters, L. (1992). *A practical guide to alternative assessment*. Alexandria, VA: Association for Supervision and Curriculum Development.

Hutchinson, F. E. (Ed.). (1945). *The works of George Herbert*. Oxford: The Clarendon Press. (See *Jacula Prudentum*.)

Johnson, D.W., & Johnson, F. P. (1991). *Joining together,* (4th ed.). Englewood Cliffs, NJ: Prentice Hall.

Kanter, R. M. (1989). *When giants learn to dance*. New York: Simon & Schuster.

Lewin, K. (1951). *Field theory in social science*. New York: Harper & Row.

Lewin, K. (1964). The mechanisms of change. In W. Bennis, E. Schein, & D. Berlew (Eds.), *Interpersonal dynamics*. Homewood, IL: Dorsey.

Lieberman, A., & Miller, L. (1990). Restructuring schools: What matters and what works. *Phi Delta Kappan, 71*(10), 759-764.

Louis, K. S., & Miles, M. B. (1990). *Improving the urban high school: What works and why*. New York: Teachers College Press

72   RESTRUCTURING SCHOOLS

Milstein, M. M. (1993). Yours, mine, and ours. *The 1993 annual for facilitators, trainers, and consultants.* San Diego, CA: Pfeiffer and Co.

Murphy, J. (1991). *Restructuring schools.* New York: Teachers College Press.

Murphy, J. (1992). *The landscape of leadership preparation.* Newbury Park, CA: Corwin Press.

National Association of Secondary School Principals. (1986). *Teacher satisfaction survey.* Reston, VA: Author.

National Commission on Excellence in Education. (1983). *A nation at risk: The imperative of educational reform.* Washington, DC: U.S. Government Printing Office.

National LEADership Network Study Group on Restructuring Schools. (1991). Washington, DC: U.S. Department of Education.

Owens, R. G. (1991). *Organization behavior in education* (4th ed.). Englewood Cliffs, NJ: Prentice-Hall.

Peters, T. J., & Waterman, R. H., Jr. (1982). *In search of excellence.* New York: Warner Books.

Pipho, C. (1992). A decade of education reform. *Phi Delta Kappan, 74*(4), 278-279.

Schein, E. H. (1986). *Organizational culture and leadership.* San Francisco: Jossey-Bass.

Schmuck, R. A., & Runkel, P. J. (1985). *The handbook of organization development in schools* (3rd ed.). Prospect Heights, IL: Waveland Press.

Shaheen, T. A., & Roberts, P. W. (1974). *School district climate improvement.* Denver: CFK.

Southwest Educational Development Laboratory (SEDL). (1990, Winter). *Issues . . . About Change, 1*(1).

Stewart, D. (1986). *The power of people skills.* New York: Wiley.

Tannenbaum, R., & Schmidt, W. H. (1958, March/April). How to choose a leadership pattern. *Harvard Business Review,* pp. 95-101.

Tuckman, B. W. (1965). Developmental sequence in small groups. *Psychological Bulletin, 63*(6), 384-399.